Maids

Abby Frucht

MATTER PRESS
Wynnewood, Pennsylvania

Maids © Abby Frucht 2020
All rights reserved
First Matter Press Edition, 2020

ISBN: 978-0-9961558-4-7

Cover design by Roma Narkhede
Interior design concept by HR Hegnauer
Text set in Gills MT

No part of this book may be reproduced or transmitted in any form or by any means, electronic or mechanical, including photocopying or recording, or by any information storage and retrieval system without permission in writing from the publisher.

MATTER PRESS
PO Box 704
Wynnewood, PA 19096
www.matterpress.com

For Syl and Liz

Every landscape reveals more of itself as you search it.
— Geoff Manaugh

MAIDS

- 1   Mirrors
- 6   Sheets
- 12   Front Porch
- 20   Much Less More
- 32   Occasionally
- 37   Broom
- 41   What Is/Was Her Name Again the Pretty Maid from Finland?
- 52   Only First
- 57   Spoons
- 59   Knives

63   Tarnish

65   Web Search

70   Cynthia

76   Train Ride w/ Apologies

MIRRORS

The first maid Ida in the button down dress that
in the website Automotive Workwear is called
a Women's Hotel Housekeeping Short Sleeve
Dress has just finished cleaning the floor length
mirror in the master bedroom of the split level
house on Harriet Lane in Huntington Long Island.

The poplin garment selling half a century later at
a discounted $19.25 might have cost Ida in 1962
a dollar and a half at the uniform store unless she
sewed it herself although not unlike the polishing
of mirrors the construction of notched collars is at
least if not more tricky than it looks.

Ida might be twenty or thirty one or forty but
maybe just eighteen. In the eyes of the doctor's
middle daughter her slender limbs and quiet
face against the crisp white collar appear to
have been polished along with the furniture as

Ida moves into the hallway her legs and arms attached to the shape of the Hotel Housekeeping Short Sleeve Dress which might appear amid the shadows to cut her off at the knees if not for the stiff white shoes she wears and at the elbows too if not for the bottle of Windex she carries and the dangling rag.

Off she goes to clean the mirrors in the rest of the house first by swiping the rag up and down on the glass then swiping it sideways and only finally at the end via widening circles completing the job never pausing to gaze at her own gleamy face the neat bobbed cap of hair the locks hemmed at the jaw line the ears not showing.

The child stepping unseen into the always dusky perfume of the master bedroom soon stands before the mirror to stick out her tongue. Soon she squashes her tongue across the expert glass and then her flat mouth greasing another spot and then another her nose and then her whole face at once her scrappy eyelashes blinking not reaching the glass no matter how she contorts. After that she steps back to examine the effect she's made on this oddly reflective all but scientific part of her environment.

She is not of the mirror.

She is not in the mirror.

She is apart from the mirror and therefore has power over the glass.

It's not the first she has exercised such an advantage since by dropping the ice cream cone onto the sidewalk she observed it break and by spilling the doctor's tall foamy stein across the just-made table so that Ida might rush forth to wipe it up she observed Ida rush forth to wipe it up since how politely the mom asks Ida to rush forth to wipe things up like if the daughter throws up the mom asks Ida would you please my apologies so Ida scrubs that too.

Or else something else happens to make the five
year old cry like Ida rushing from the hallway
taking hold of the child and scolding her for
smearing a morning's work such as why do you
ruin my pretty new mirror so the child too howls
so soon the mom steps in on doughy doctor's
wife ankles so the child still sniffling is led to
the kitchen and fed juice from a cup which she
empties by drinking although she never thinks of
cups as being part of her environment subject to
her power to make them different.

Next week Ida never comes back. I had to
fire the cleaning lady does yours have time for
another Wednesday the mom asks of several
other doctors' wives on the phone one morning.
Now what does that mean? Fire the cleaning
lady? The child pictures a torch the notched
collar igniting the durable weave of the fabric
melting she sees the flapping of the rag the

kicked blue Windex someone's mouth wide open
against the glass.

SHEETS

The second maid Della less slender than Ida not so graceful in her movements from room to room slides her comfortable body between the two twin beds in the master bedroom in order to strip them and smooth on fresh sheets.

Not infrequently she talks with the child while cleaning the clumsy introverted middle girl who talks too much although at other times Della chats amiably enough with the missus like if it's time to fix lunch the missus always reading books or preparing something special for supper in advance such a funny chef she is arriving home from Jeff's seafood with sacks of lobsters for the family or on other days Swanson's in foil trays.

Della's legs in thick stockings scritch sideways between two shoved apart mattresses since instead of one bed the doctor's wife and the

doctor sleep on two twin beds under not one
but two fitted sheets pressed neatly together
under one top sheet so no one can tell. Static
slaps against the ceiling as Della flips open one
twin sheet and then another and then the big
sheet on top. The middle child the clumsy talker
so unlike the older daughter who chats with her
friends and stays busy somewhere emerges from
the bathroom the master bath where Candy
the dog falls asleep sometimes such as inside
the glassed in shower stall such as if one of the
daughters traps it there Candy simply lays down
on the cool scrubbed tile thumping its tail.

The middle daughter brings an odor of poop
with her out of the bathroom although here
in this house with the doctor father they call
poop BM even the children call it that. You wash
your hands Della calls? The child says yes. So
lemme see Della calls tugging hard at the three
sheets smoothing the contours soon fetching six
pillowcases nothing pretty about them she says

to herself but is that okay to put? To put words in her thoughts into words into Della?

The child sidles backward into the bathroom there's a sound of running water the swip of a towel the towel will need to be hung back up again. So lemme see Della calls. So now the child glides forward hands stiff against the front of her the girl is frightened of static the way it hides amid the sheets jumps out with a crackle that really does hurt. Taking two small hands into her big hands Della rotates each finger but never brusquely only greeting the tips with her soft deft round ones. Good job she affirms. Still the child sidles further between the two beds which share just one headboard so that the beds pushed apart in a V for bed-making make between them one V so when the child sidles nearer into the V she and Della squish up into one squished person.

The little girl turned six a week ago.

You can tell sometimes when she gets near
speaking the child works her utterances more
carefully than you might think and for that reason
you develop a habit of preparing to answer her
mindfully but in a manner still fit for a child's ears
as would a governess or nanny for instance if
the girl asks what's the dif between a governess
and a nanny Della answers difference. Also
governesses live in fancier houses fancier than
this one although this one is bigger than the
house they moved out of as are the trees all up
and down Wedgewood Lane a road with only
three houses too many trees and yet another
dog Kato living next door the size of two fire
trucks. At last the girl opens her mouth to speak.
It's the color of your skin she says.

Della told me you said something mean to her
the mom says next week when Della never
comes back. The four of them are in the car
the mom and three daughters the two other
daughters not listening. The car is stopped at

the light at Jericho Turnpike while traveling most likely to Miracle Mile to buy the pink dress with the wide brown sash for the middle daughter the mod paisley A-line dress for the older daughter the aproned dress for the younger. One day the older girls will receive their first sex talk at just this intersection the doctor's wife in the driver's seat facing the road the sisters in the back seat regarding her knuckles pink against the steering wheel the facets blinking here and there among the four or five rings the dad buys for her birthdays. Someday boys will want to touch your nipples maybe even kiss them but you shouldn't ever let them but then the light turns green so that's the end of the sex talk which is a good thing.

I didn't mean to says the daughter.

You didn't mean to say the mean thing or you didn't mean it to be mean?

To be mean the girl answers.

The light changes just then so the car gets moving the mom allows from now on remember think before you speak and say you're sorry apologize. I'm not sorry thinks the girl I was thinking she thinks and for years she will feel as if misunderstood about it and still the question remains nearly sixty years later did Della not come back because Della wished not to or was Della let go as the mom came to call it the daughter can't ask the mom and dad both dead the static startles the bedspread atop her one bed to make it look like two beds to lie down on together.

FRONT PORCH

For some years after her marriage is over the doctor's daughter lives on Main Street in a house she loved for its broad front porch. The porch isn't a wraparound. The house is too cozy and small for a wraparound but she enjoys that too about it its just rightness for just one single mom she can scrub it dust it sweep it sponge it mop it no problem her boys helping out maybe though probably not but the tidy modest cube of it the shutters on the windows and in the big picture window a BB hole she likes since when her boys put their fingers on the starbursted glass they can feel no broken part just the inner pane unbroken there's a metaphor there only she's not saying.

She likes sitting on the porch wearing one of her long flowing post divorce skirts reading books or writing thoughts on her students' weekly packets while drinking pomegranate sun tea iced in a jar.

Let's say it's '96 maybe '7 she's forty or so she'll
need to have the hysterectomy three years later
and then the breast cancer too will make rather
a mess of some parts of her self but for now she
is whole just out of her marriage her body whole
her self freshly unbothered.

There's a redneck sort of guy she digs who
works for Wisconsin Public Service who once
showed up at the house to check for carbon
monoxide fumes in the basement but she has
never expressed her interest in him she hasn't
even caught sight of him in four or five months
not even in the trucks the big Wisconsin Public
Service Trucks lurching by.

She sits drinking red tea on the porch one day
when a black man who passes now and then on
the sidewalk and calls up at her to wonder how
are you doing this fine afternoon or where are
your sweet little babies today finally stops on
his way past the house to say excuse me pretty

lady may I join you on that porch? She answers
sure c'mon up. Black men have a nicer more
interesting way of coming on to ladies than white
men do she knows from where she used to live
in Oberlin Ohio. Like if a white guy mumbles um
so would you mind if I like help you load those bags
into your trunk a black guy says wish I had that
swing in my back yard and if a white guy says um
like maybe I can carry them into the parking lot
for you a black guy steps up in the middle of the
aisle saying hey can you tell me where they keep
the honey in here?

There's a loveseat on the porch and two
Adirondacks the less rotten of which is the
chair in which she's sitting so he slides into the
other more spongy Adirondack to tell her his
name although now that their proximity is finally
established it's clear at once to both of them
he's too young for her by decades she could be
his professor all her papers books tea on the
stool between them a pen disappeared amid

the folds of her skirt she remembers that skirt
even decades later the way she dropped stuff in
it forgot what stuff was kept there shared stuff
from within it gave stuff away.

Still they chat for a while to be polite about
living in Oshkosh Wisconsin and which cities
they'll choose if they leave here for elsewhere
and how here on Main Street you need to shut
the windows tight in order for the house to stay
quiet enough to even talk on the phone and how
high the road floods after the rain so high the
Salvation Army drove round afterwards once
to hand out bottled water so the kid next door
hung over the porch rail with his tongue sticking
out like he'd passed away of thirst in the exact
opposite of the nick of time. That neighbor family
is the Geins she tells her visitor so to everyone
they meet they always start out by saying not
that Gein we're not related meaning not Ed Gein
the Butcher of Plainfield seventy six miles south
of here on U.S. 100 who murdered two or more

people and fashioned keepsakes from the skins bones hair and fingernails of exhumed corpses. Still she hasn't so much as offered her visitor iced tea yet when one of the big Wisconsin Public Service trucks wheezes up at the curb.

It isn't possible yet since Main Street isn't widened yet for big trucks to park at the curb without blocking traffic so ordinarily the trucks yaw into the driveways but this one lurches to the curb and when the door swings open out jumps the guy she hasn't laid eyes on since he tested the basement for carbon monoxide the redneck sort of guy she digs but well read since he had paused to admire her bookshelves even poetry even books she is holding for when her boys grow up even books she's never read cook books her dead mom's scribbled notes in the margins such as sweet not salted such as cut by half and other books she's never opened books she'll hang onto for maybe years later such as maybe if she takes them down when she is sixty which for the record she is but she hasn't she might find she'll grow fond of moved by attached to some things she finds written there.

The white guy's crew cut anyway is one of the things she digs about him since her ex wore a pony tail. Crew Cut leaps up the porch steps and says you ok? She answers sure thanks I'm fine. Okay then I just want to make sure you're good he repeats not glancing at her visitor in the rotting Adirondack glancing only at her but not meeting her eyes which is exactly how he didn't when he checked on the leak in the basement either. Then off he bounds down the porch steps gets back in his Wisconsin Public Service truck and is driven away since he isn't the driver there's another crew cut in there he must have said to him pull over I gotta check on this lady something looks I don't know I gotta see if she's okay with it.

Not long after that her visitor Jerome she

remembers his name even twenty years later says goodbye and strolls away down the sidewalk the afro she still calls it she doesn't know the new word for it if there is a new word or two or three words for it frosty with light above the squared off shoulders the tee shirt loose but well fitting strumming a breeze. She tells herself maybe Jerome doesn't know. She supposes this in earnest. For days she makes herself suppose it. She tells herself probably I'm the only one of the two of us me and Jerome who caught on to what exactly was happening here the hole from where the BB burst in the glass not a cutting sort of sharp but not a metaphor either. Either that or it was me being older me being older than him being nearly his great grandma's age that did it caused Jerome to walk away never passing along on the sidewalk again since he's moved to Chicago Green Bay Milwaukee Bloomington Minneapolis Champagne or St Louis.

But have we spoken of how romantic the

doctor's daughter is in those post-divorce
years her blousy skirts making practically
everything including motherhood yardwork even
housecleaning sexual? She props her feet on
the loveseat noting for the hundredth time the
wicker being made not of wicker but plastic.
But it looks like wicker.

MUCH LESS MORE

The two of them the doctor's daughter now
60 and Kayla the dog cross Rosalia Street at
Woodchucks Bar & Grill. The lab is muzzled
because she comes to their home from a
crapshoot history. Not even the Humane Society
shelter can say what wrongs the dog committed
to have been exiled there though she's been
pretty much a lady ever since Chuck brought
her home. She even crosses her legs when she
lies down all four pretty ankles entwined at once
and when she steps off the sidewalk she looks
like somebody modeling a bathing suit testing the
water.

Woodchucks used to be called the Sit n'Stay and
before that General Lee's but the same guys hold
up the bench outside waiting not impatiently
though hardly anything does except the little
blonde girl who lives in the neighborhood who

always falls down for something worthy of their
forbearance of it to happen that day. There's a
tavern nearby called Mike & Sue's and sometimes
Kayla snoops at that landing as if sniffing out
the pros and cons of stealing back where she
came from like maybe Mike and Sue are the folks
who dumped her but when she ambles past
Woodchucks she cold shoulders the guys in their
caps on the bench her slender face inside the
muzzle reminding the doctor's daughter of fists
in brass the tender knuckles fortified.

From the opposite curb steps a school boy.

Since there aren't many black people here in
Oshkosh Wisconsin it's not impossible the dog
has never crossed paths with a single much
less more dark skinned person in all the walks
she's ever taken in her nine or ten years. Plus
the schoolboy's a kid Kayla dislikes kids at least
according to the shelter which provided no
evidence only a warning plus the daughter can't

exactly avoid the boy walk away cross over or start back home in the other direction.

The doctor's daughter depresses the retracting button meaning to undo the slack on the leash but by mistake releasing it startling even Kayla though it appears to be only the dog's canine self that concerns her. Like when her hackles go up it makes her pause to observe what the rest of her not dog self might be gearing up to do about it.

Good Dog preempts the daughter let's call the doctor's daughter Alf since that's what the doctor dad used to call her in fondly humorous regard of her middle initial and the Pixie Cut she hated. She tugs the leash a little closer wishing she was walking their puppy instead Kayla's dumb younger brother who cartwheels around because he misconstrues leashes as being of God God being Dog backwards which is why they yank him backwards which terrifies him. But Kayla carries herself past the center of the road as the boy too steps nearer. What he means is to pet and commune with the dog but that this boy doesn't always get what he wants may be gleaned from the caliber of his approach the way he tethers each longing at the end of its leash like his mom must have taught him.

Beyond the curb squats a house one of the chewed on by time looking bungalows with lattice skirting to which flotsam clings. The old windows are clean and the mom might just this minute squint past the warped glass to where the three of them bony lady yellow dog boy in gargantuan micro suede footwear will cross paths in one second or worse collide. More than once through this same window can be seen that girl falling the small kid with blonde bangs who lives just past the corner it's the most disturbing sight but hilarious too since the girl never keeps on lying there. She'll be standing around throwing hopscotch with her friends then at once tip over backwards when no one's near enough to

catch her maybe something inner ear-ish maybe
something poltergeist-ish unless she means to
right the planet correct for the species' graver
imbalance. The girl's friends pay no mind to
these drop attacks unless she ends up blocking
a hopscotch square. Or they'll be gathered in
the yard the freckled girl and her playmates just
talking maybe trading spoonerisms griping making
plans until the dinner hour assigning parts in a
game about moth men maybe but soon again the
tippy child tips straight over backwards onto the
grass the trammeled poorly mown lawn holding
clumps of tattered peonies being the thing she
entrusts with catching her after which she lies
still so as to keep in check the wobble of the
galaxy or maybe only watching clouds before by
making some adjustments you can't make head or
tail of except for pigtails swaying she bounces up
again.

May I please pet your dog the boy inquires
rather formally since not a wheeler dealer type

he is nevertheless inclined to negotiate. His piano fingers levitate so Kayla glides underneath them acquiescing to the posture expected of her. Not being the sort of dog who takes for granted the kindness of just anybody Kayla yields circumspectly to the boy's gallant up and down patting the kind of petting people do when the word pet is their sole directive. It's even possible the boy has never once petted a dog before his mom flinching on the opposite pane of the window blaming all eventualities on the lady with the leash supposing maybe he'll get bitten maybe he'll demand his own animal maybe he'll bawl since he's not above bawling he's only ten only not around strangers in which case he's a gentleman as he has been taught or rather commanded. His mom keeps track of all the many ways she grooms him protects him his bearing limp yet balletic his sad handsome smile.

As much as Kayla has crossed maybe no other paths with black people hardly has Alf the

doctor's daughter either here in Wisconsin
although she wishes it might someday be
otherwise such as let's say she gets a job
downtown a normal workaday job such as typing
in an office she might find a black friend or at
least know someone's name enough to come
to some kind of fond attachment such as maybe
meeting early for breakfast some days it really
pains her some days like not even when Alf was
a girl on Long Island did she make black friends
since not including all the cleaning ladies Ida
Della and Nell who was Grandma Dorothy's
who screeched if you laid your jacket on the
floor you throw your jacket on the floor and
then you wear it? except you didn't call Dorothy
Grandma you called her just Dorothy and also
most certainly including Cynthia who lived
upstairs on Wedgewood Lane in the little room
whose ten year old daughter Wanda the doctor's
daughter's same age who wished to be a doctor
lived with her dad far away in The Grenadines but
not including the white cleaning ladies Martha

from Hungary who didn't shave her armpits
and whatever her name was with red hair from
Finland the only black people the doctor's
daughter practically ever laid eyes on when she
was a kid was the girl in junior high school who
shouted Hey Chicken Legs if they passed at the
lockers and a second grade kid at Flower Hill
Elementary who got bullied so bad he laid his
head on his desk cloaked his face in his sleeves
and soon was moved to the class with the kids
all in wheelchairs who couldn't speak and too a
naked boy framed by a doorway at camp whose
penis confused her nearly forever by being
abnormal until she realized in her twenties he
was uncut the sole uncircumcised she'd glimpsed
in the flesh up close in person and even now
remains so.

Oh and too of course the garbage men except
they only made noise you couldn't see them
when they worked they came and went in the
dark.

How old the boy asks?

You play piano Alf asks?

The boy ignores this question. Alf tells him the vet guesses Kayla's maybe nine maybe ten or eleven so athletic you could diagram her muscles just by telling her to stay.

What kind?

Yellow lab.

What's his name?

She's a she Alf says. And then since Kayla's name embarrasses her such as Brandi might or Tammy she explains the name was Kayla when they found her at the shelter. The new puppy is Truman she tells him explaining all Chuck's dogs have been named for U.S. presidents just as all Alf's dogs when Alf was growing up weren't Candy to which the boy only thoughtfully strokes Kayla's muzzle then lifts up an ear to let it slide from his fingers as Kayla aims her gaze to where the same shaggy eagle has built the same jagged nest in the same bald tree as in Aprils before.

In his neat pressed button down blue checked shirt the boy maintains that solemn well mannered comportment that makes her wonder how it came to be Easter already without her knowing. After this she won't see him ever again. She'll know it's not him because she'll see no black kid on this road again ever not even at the middle school polling station on election days where if there ever is a black kid she might mistake that other black kid for this same boy might launch into a fond befuddled reunion the squatting bungalow vacant the glass no longer scrubbed and no one squinting from the window.

Okay then but what does she cost he asks meaning either how much did they pay for Kayla

or what are they willing to sell her for? All dogs
cost different amounts Alf answers finessing both
questions for instance Kayla's a rescue dog but the
puppy Truman's a pedigree that means we know
his parents also too we asked the breeder for the
cuddliest puppy so that's what Truman is. How much
did Truman cost? Enough she says. A lot she deflects.
How much the boy asks there comes a flick at the
glass like it's time for the boy to come in and set
the supper table.

The boy's mom lost her footing once washing
a window. The doctor's daughter once on
Valentine's slid onto her bottom on ice on the
sidewalk while starting out for Piggly Wiggly to
buy one rose for herself and a second for her
friend another recent divorcee who couldn't
afford to buy flowers that year not so much as a
fistful of dandelions. For Kayla we paid the shelter
thirty five dollars she answers truthfully this
time at which the boy doesn't blink. His mom's
breath fogs the glass soon she'll wipe at the

pane with a Brawny towel. The doctor's daughter
doesn't know what to call herself. The bench
at Woodchucks Bar and Grill sits empty now
and the funny thing is that neither woman will
ever catch sight of the blonde girl who always
falls down again. Such as maybe she grows up
or simply stops falling. Her repair of the planet
despite her efforts postponed. Even so it appears
there might be some hope left for when the boy
says see you Alf reaches. They shake.

OCCASIONALLY

Occasionally what irks her is the question of syllables since doctor's daughter has too many while she has too few not to mention commas bug her because they cause a divide between halves of a thought parts of a recollection figments of emotion no less irksome than mosquitoes they buzz in the middles of things they have no business punctuating and in addition similes.

Plus I doesn't work since of course there are others who feeling as she does experience similar worries dogs street names whiteness histories fusterclucks and polling places not to mention this fug of mortified shyness she can't stand in herself when she's around black people a déjà vu of vexed embarrassment like of the books in the house when she was a girl the mom's books in the hundreds including just two the doctor's

daughter was forbidden to open Eldridge
Cleaver's Soul on Ice and Malcolm X's autobiography
books she still hasn't read although she purchased
both once and keeps them near on a shelf but feels
unequal to making contact with them.

It was said the books would frighten her.

Give the daughter bad dreams.

Also is it wrong to hope to imagine Cynthia's
feelings? To put words into her thoughts into hopes
in her as people might scold to put speech in her
in hoping not to leave her speechless but in the
end to very possibly but not at all meaning to in
fact wishing not to appropriate Cynthia? Cynthia
who cried? Whose reedy clarinet voice squeaked
when she cried? Who lived upstairs in the little
room? Who hung her Women's Hotel Housekeeping
Short Sleeve Dresses in the closet off the
playroom with the vacuum cleaner in it?
Who wasn't permitted to go to church? Who

didn't speak aloud of that and other certain observations? Who kept her daughter Wanda's dreams in the pockets of her dresses the blue airmail from Saint Vincent and the Grenadines folded handkerchief style? Who was fired/let go because she wept because she was homesick because she missed her own daughter the doctor's daughter's same age? Who even now five decades later might feel in her bones someone's thinking of me somebody remembers unfolding my letters my letters to Charles my letters to Wanda their letters to me only who she might ask who's thinking of the maid who hopes to imagine putting thoughts into rhymes into hopes in me?

It was said to be a kindness.

To let Cynthia go was the way the mom put it.

A kindness to let her.

To let her to send her to let her go back.

Who wept in the playroom when Bobby
Kennedy was buried while keeping both hands
on the sewing machine for the arranging of the
fabric for the dining room curtains the watery
deep blue floating petals the two pleated blue
skirts made of just one remnant.

Also is it pathetic to hope to imagine Wanda
Cynthia's daughter decades later at sixty the
doctor's daughter's exact same age a surgeon in
scrubs at some sink in some hospital enacting
Hand Hygiene in Health Care Guidelines having
got what she dreamed of or rather earned
her degree paid for it the way her mother too
wept for it was let go by the doctor's daughter's
mother for weeping too much for it who maybe
despaired of it?

Plus a cousin once wondered do you keep a clean
house like Liz does? Liz the nutritionist being the
youngest of the three doctor's daughters who

lives on E. 72nd Street New York City. Liz of two
Murphy beds a kitchen the size of a toaster oven.
Come to think of it yes says the doctor's daughter
who removes from her floors all beans macaronis
other comma shaped sweepings the bright snips
of spilled rosemary sage you can't tell which it is
once it drops to the floor only sometimes she
sifts it back into the jars such as burrs off the dogs
during pheasant hunting season in the jars when
she's cooking although last time she'd visited Liz's
apartment she hadn't thought of the clean floor in
such exact terms never thought of Liz sweeping
mopping and dusting nor regarded the neat folded
sweaters in dry cleaner bags on shelves in the
closet as effects Liz was having on her environment.
Must instead in her mind have invented tall figures
wearing Women's Hotel Housekeeping Short Sleeve
Dresses floating in through the single high corner
Manhattan window their postures bending to allow
them into the room their eyes dry their eyes deep
in their pockets.

BROOM

In the eyes of the dog Kayla's dumb younger brother the puppy Truman it appears the doctor's daughter is making an effort to undo a wrong.

Night upon night the same undoing.

First she takes up the thing drags the head along floorboards swiping and towing maybe dancing but Truman mistrusts dancing fears the floor twisting open fears her needing his saviorship. He's afraid of the thing. He fears it will smite her. The furtive labors she takes with it pawing the floorboards his own dander his own molecules snurfed up by its whiskers along with bits of purest earth the cleanest splinters of the planet the smited no see ums.

It's past Truman's bedtime he'll have bad dreams.

Puppies do.

Chuck and Kayla have already climbed upstairs.

Still Truman won't leave her alone in this scuffle
instead he crouches as near as he dares at
least it's not the thing that roars the thing that
rumbles and fumes the stupid endless long tail
of it thrown round her ankles. It appears she
must cast all furies aside to contend with the
thing night upon night the long neck unyielding.
He hopes she won't fall down. Dog being God
backwards he prays she won't cry. She's not the
kind of human who never cries. Too he worries
he'll fail her and be himself smited his eyes
trashed his tail smudged his ears cast to the
floorboards while still the head stays put the
thing's neck unvanquishable the raspy stubble not
quivering. It's the thing he believes she is tussling
with not the thought behind the spine of it the no
ears eyes or mouth of it not the daughter's
recollections of being a girl not expected to sweep

instead was given one job that of trimming the
hedges in exchange for dollars it was the only task
she knew she wasn't expected to do it too well
oh too setting tables although she shared that task
with the older and younger of her two sisters one
spoons one forks one knives the napkins shared
among the three of them the dog Candy Truman's
second great granddog once removed's water bowl
filled each day three times by the three of them. Five
forks on the table one fork Cynthia's on the counter
facing away from them into the kitchen five
knives on the table one knife Cynthia's on the
counter facing away from them into the kitchen
six spoons same way napkins too the crumbs
swept off the counter two handed by Cynthia
when dinner was done the empty table swept
too once the chairs were all empty two-handed
by Cynthia the chairs swept too the dog Candy's
bowl rinsed with fresh tap water.

Truman labors past bedtime holding open his
eyes not daring to blink his long ears quivering

the spilled macaronis the kidneys commas and lentils she doesn't speak she won't swear she casts her fury her repentance her delinquency aside the thing is taller than she is when she bends down but soon she wrestles the thing back into its closet nails it up by its neck dumps the snurfings in the trash it lets her go it lets her climb upstairs to bed.

The floor remains where it belongs.

Truman is hero.

Night upon night he succeeds in this.

WHAT IS/WAS HER NAME AGAIN THE PRETTY MAID FROM FINLAND

Such a lovely name she has/had the lovely new
maid from Finland who is/was/ had/has a fiancé/e.
Because she is/was fair. Because she eats/ate no
sugar. Because she drinks a lot of milk. Because
she had red hair. Because she is slender with long
red hair. Because she eats/ate no Chunky Good
& Plenty M&M Tootsie Pop Mary Jane or Sugar
Daddy. Because she ate no pies her face tranquil
as teacups of such vivid translucence you could/
can see yourself in it. Because she has no freckles
just one beauty mark of which she is/was self
conscious calls it a blemish you aren't allowed
to mention how pretty it looks says the doctor's
daughter's mom to her friends Iris Irving and Amy
Ann Bloomgarten on the telephone the other
doctors' wives with maids and cleaning ladies not
so lucky not from Finland also daughters of their
own.

She's engaged to a young man from Cold Spring Harbor I don't know maybe something to do with horses the fishery the hatchery maybe even a biologist I don't know how long she'll stay I'm afraid not very.

Because she eats not even Welch's has never tasted Kool Aid if you offer her Kool Aid she blushes you can watch her turn pink. Yes. Very pleasant to have in the house on Wednesdays she has Tuesdays available never Thursdays since her fiancé takes her to lunch on Thursdays.

It's not impossible so far that the doctor's daughter's mom Alice/Carolyn comes off unappealing but really she is/was loved and deservedly admired. For her soy kumquat chicken her modesty her sharp witted daily reading of the New York Times hundreds of biographies novels her not ostentatious living room couch of a mustard yellow velvet her even not ostentatious wearing of rings her kindness

to saleswomen waitresses seamstresses the new
ball gown hemmed too short but she paid for it
anyway never griping at the seamstress that the
fabric reaches not quite all the way down never
ended up wearing the stylish gown doesn't/didn't
want to hurt the other woman's seamstress
feelings wore the old pink gauzy chiffon gown
instead but with the topaz rings such a witty
combination.

Also the magazine clippings hidden in a hatbox
on a high up shelf in the master bedroom closet
depicting a clothing model who in the very
same gown looked nearly just like her but with
a not surprisingly somewhat trimmer rear end.
You couldn't look at the clippings unless you
ask/asked at which point there would/will be a
production made the unfolding of the ritual step
ladder the bequesting of the hatbox the prayerful
sighs all around oh you really do Carolyn you do
you look just like the clothing model except for
her Caroline you do she looks just like you Alice

since Carolyn was once called Alice since Alice used to be her name but which people mistook for Caroline since that was/is the more usual spelling. Except for the rear end. For instance when Alice/Carolyn/Caroline enrolled at Adelphi University in Garden City she needed once to stand in line holding records of her self/selves in the school nurse folder. So she opened the folder to peek at the words that the school nurse had written. Alice is a skinny yellow girl the nurse had written.

After which Alice changed her name to Carolyn who was/is kind to saleswomen seamstresses waitresses except for maybe when letting go/firing the maids such as Cynthia being sent back to Saint Vincent no longer to earn even half enough dollars to send her daughter dear Wanda one day to medical school it was only because poor Cynthia was so unhappy wept so many tears missed her daughter her husband her church so much it was a kindness really to let her go. Plus the doctor too was kindly was/is gentle was/is loved smoothed a cloth atop the table and sat whittlng animals in his evening hours the curled shavings of pine maple cedar wafting to the carpet from where he sat in his chair in the conjuring of anteaters pelicans storks the broken foot of the bullfrog affixed with a peg no wider around than the circumference of a sewing needle so all these many decades later when the doctor's daughter now sixty dusts the gentle dad Howard's animals on her fireplace mantel and bends to rescue the broken fallen off frog foot she regards the foot a moment in the palm of her hand grieves a moment texts one of her sisters guess what I'm holding in the palm of my hand then pins the broken frog together again.

Also for speaking her mind the doctor's wife Carolyn is/was admired such as if someone said something racist and bad and objectionable Alice/Caroline/Carolyn often could be counted on to speak out albeit nervously but firmly her voice trembling against the firmness of it. For instance once Aunt Stella said but when I got back to the telephone the caller was gone. Of course he didn't say he was he wouldn't why would he but I could tell by the sound of his voice he was by how he sounded when he asked is the house still available he was but all I said was excuse me for just one minute I need to get this same meatloaf we're eating out of the oven but when I got back he'd fled he had hung up the phone he was extremely polite he was very well spoken I felt/feel lousy about it except I have to imagine it's best for the neighbors.

To which the doctor's wife Carolyn/Caroline/Alice said Stella really I can't believe what I'm hearing to which Stella asked what to which Caroline/Carolyn/Alice answered nothing come to think of it even now when the doctor's daughter half a century later sits hoping to remember the mom didn't/doesn't speak her mind firmly against it but in the car on the way home from meatloaf at Aunt Stella's she did

speak her mind like at the stoplight for as long
as it stayed red at the intersection and also
too other times and also too in downtown
Huntington when the younger sister Liz asked
what's that when a black man stepped/steps out
of the Partyland store the doctor's wife blushing
answered darling that's a man.

Oh but Madleen/Maktaleena/Marceline/Madelen
the very pretty maid from Finland engaged
to be married to a handsome young eligible
meteorologist/botonist/icthyologist/zoologist/
entomologist from Cold Spring Harbor because
she has/had perfect skin you could drink it.

And do you know they have a system the maids a
secret network Carolyn/Caroline/Alice tells her
friends Iris Irving and Amy Ann Bloomgarten and
Bonnie Gellinger they have a network the maids
they pose as one another's references they pose
as employers they pose as their own employers
they pose as you and me they pretend to be

us speaking for and about them even though
they are not. Because when I was calling for
references this morning I spoke to the same girl
the same voice I spoke with last week when last
week I called to interview a new girl I ended
up speaking with the same girl the same voice
about whom I got the reference for another
yet another girl the week before. Last week.
This morning. They're crafty these girls I have to
admire them but at the same time shouldn't we
find it insulting? Don't they realize somebody will
figure them out? At least they never pretend to
be doctors' wives they pretend to be engineers'
wives at Grumman don't they realize Grumman
is going under closing down all the engineers out
of their lifelong jobs we bought our Compton's
Encyclopedia from one of the engineers last
week he was sad to see it go he needed to sell it
we regretted being the ones to pay him for it we
paid him extra for it more than he was asking for
it.

In a way I suppose I admire their nerve do you
admire it too the maids pretending to be us
speaking for them on the telephones if this was
Mary Poppins it would be funny but in a way I
do envy it admire it am fond of them for it said/
says Caroline/Alice/Caroline who when she was
skinny and yellow a schoolgirl resembled in her
bafflement sketches of Alice Pleasance Hargreaves
born Alice Liddell aka Alice down the rabbit hole
after which she changed her name to the more
elegant but kindly Carolyn who in the eyes of her
daughter the doctor's middle daughter is only
sometimes and in relation to only some things
clueless Caroline since what she never did realize
or if she did ever realize never did say is that it
hurt it must have hurt it must have made her
meaning Cynthia more homesick than before to
be sat facing into the kitchen to gaze at the meat
slicer the sliced tongue slicer since that's what
Jewish people ate/eat some nights for supper
instead of sitting with the girls and the doctor
and his wife at the table discussing how they'd

passed the day such as how did you pass the day
Cynthia oh yes thank you for asking I polished
the ladles it was such a bright morning the sun
made me sneeze except instead she sat facing
into the kitchen the giant blender gleaming only if
properly cleaned not so much if it's not she can/
could not see her own face in it.

For instance Caroline/Alice/Carolyn kept/keeps
the house keys hidden the older sister the older
daughter Syl the judge remembers she never
let the maids have them even Cynthia who lived
there whose bedroom was the little room if
on Thursdays if she ever went out needed only
ring the bell in order to have the door opened/
open to her said Carolyn on the telephone the
older daughter remembers except she never
did Cynthia she never did go out but maybe
because she was given no key. For instance what
if they have/had boyfriends? For instance if the
boyfriends in a way or even many ways or even
half a way are not recommendable said Caroline

or in some ways many maybe even one way tarnished?

In case of which you shouldn't.

Ever give the girls keys.

Except for Madelen/Madleen/Maktaleena/Marceline the pretty as milk maid from Finland who was given a key to be kept in a purse/tote/pocketbook with Madelen/Madleen/Marceline/Makteleena's name on it.

ONLY FIRST

Also is it wrong to hope to imagine what the mother the doctor's wife Carolyn/Alice/Caroline maybe penned in the margins of Soul on Ice for instance or of The Autobiography of Malcolm X? Was it maybe the comments that had been penned in the margins by the mother the doctor's wife Alice/Caroline/Carolyn when she was no longer skinny and yellow the thing that the daughter had been not allowed to read since it would give her bad dreams? Or was it the text itself the words that were printed there on the pages that had been written there by Cleaver and X that had been published there made final there the thing that would give the middle daughter bad dreams? Or was it both maybe both that would give or maybe neither?

Yes maybe neither the words that been printed on the pages nor the marks the mom had penned there or both would give the daughter bad dreams. In which case mom might be the one to dream instead. For so late she sometimes stayed in her bed on occasional if not so terribly frequent mornings the twin bed matched with the dad's twin bed the box springs mated the big sheet tucked up as one proper marriage bed well into some mornings Caroline/Alice/Carolyn her puffy ankles tucked sideways under the covers her thin nightgown riding up the events going on in the rest of the house such as soap bubbles popping in mop buckets steam hissing in the iron the feather duster whisking along on the spines not even the Electrolux causing enough of a ruckus to wake her.

Such as !!!. Such as { }. Such as -oh- and -yes- and -no- and -oh no- and -agreed-. Such as [ ]. The mom's scribblings in the margins in cursive in ballpoint not fountain such as favored by the doctor the sweet natured Howard with his ex Libris labels the mom's name not included.

Whatever's written in books you believe the doctor Howard advised. If it's printed in books in newspapers magazines typeset on bound or come to think of it not necessarily bound pages believe it if it's not don't.

Only why so obedient why didn't the daughter on occasional mornings such as if the mom was still in bed or somewhere out in her car or having lunch with her friends Iris Irving and Deena Shoemaker and Bonnie Finkelstein and Beatrice Judith Oppenheimer why didn't the daughter simply walk to the study sneak those books off the shelf open them up and for once read them? Yes why such a mama's girl why so obedient? It was a kindness to forbid her. To not give her bad dreams. Of Soul on Ice it was written in Kirkus Reviews "with remarkable assurance and without most of the mannerisms of a – much less – Negro – as when he overrates – will embarrass even – violently – white women's – may end up." And in the New York Times of

Malcolm X's assassination the doctor's wife surely
read or may have read if even on the triangle
hats made of newspaper folded and creased by
the visiting cousin Robin's cleaning lady Paca who
couldn't write or read herself "on Feb. 21 1965 –
only 39 – about to address – many death threats
– doesn't frighten – no one can get out."

Such as ????? Such as ?????????
Because the question marks the mom's question
marks penned in the margins resembling can-can
girls always in multiples and also the interestings
the trues the maybes and extraordinaries solo if
more complicated.

Only too it must be mentioned certain songs
made Caroline/Carolyn/Alice cry the only time
the three daughters ever saw her cry such as
has anybody here seen my old friend John/
Martin/Abraham/Bobby. Like if that happened
to be playing on the speakers on occasion if the
radio was turned up loud enough for how warm

under the covers on not very often occasional
mornings all curled up sideways the pretty straps
of the new nightgown the middle daughter
climbing in to pluck and strum and snuggle there.

SPOONS

Today's task is to polish what wasn't polished last
week including the dessert forks the dinner forks
lobster forks cheese fork fruit fork serving forks
fish and prosciutto forks also roast pork fork
which is a funny thing to say the name you try
not to call it but some mornings you do and so
does she the doctor's wife at which both of you
howl but at the table that night the guests laugh
hardest instead about the joke concerning fruit
the funny unfamiliar fruit you never saw before
that night you halve it with a blade scoop out the
juicy innards using a spoon then spoon the juicy
innards into a bowl then throw away the rest
then carry high the pretty bowl into the room
with the guests to set the bowl on the table the
serving fork and serving spoon balanced inside
amid sugary green pale skeins of fruit a spilled
necklace of beads but you have thrown away
the edibles the parts they like to eat not the pail

the machine has already gobbled all the parts
they like to eat which makes the funniest joke
you need to admit so you laugh when it's told at
other doctors' wives' dinner parties wherever
whenever melon is served you always know
when that joke will be told again.

KNIVES

The spoons knives forks ladles tongs and other serving tools reside in a box lined in velvet unless only mere felt it's not easy to say the felt being so soft anyway. So too the velvet couch in the living room so hard at the beginning to keep straight dear Wanda the many walled and ceilinged rooms study den play dining kitchen dressing even laundry with not enough elbow room for such a tall lady your mother me Cynthia ironing.

The dog Candy resides when the weather turns warm in the laundry room Wanda or in the kitchen where the floor remains cool and then in winter ambles off to reside where the carpet is soft in the living room except for sometimes in the bathroom there are too many rooms the walk-in closet the shower stall the dog Candy flops down being led there by one of the doctor's daughters the dog doesn't complain the dog just flops down to snore there.

The carpet in the living room is made of some fiber not real but soft anyway. The playroom curtains so too the drapes in the living room made of fibers made of glass that when you straighten and smooth them put glass in your fingers unless you remember to put on gloves. I didn't sew those glass curtains Charles they were sewn by a lady residing downtown across the park from the cemetery where on some days the daughters play with their friends they like to act out orphans on top of the graves. The middle daughter likes to help me to put on rubber gloves likes to hold the gloves open while I push my fingers into them likes to wonder do they fit likes to rub her own fingers along the folds of the drapes to feel the stinging of the glass she has no household chores Charles only sometimes makes her bed. The youngest daughter not the middle is the cutest of the sisters the most pure of the doctor's three daughters she likes

to tuck their mother's reading glasses under her
chin then pretend to be a person named Mrs.
Fa. The insides of the tines of the salad forks are
tarnished Charles. The insides of the petals of
the roses on the handles of the spoons inside
the box lined in velvet if it's velvet are tarnished
who is thinking these things these fifty years later
putting things into words into thoughts in me
Charles? So too is the ladle but there's a cloth
made of felt made for rubbing the unshiny parts
away although you need to wear gloves so that
the stench of the polish won't ruin your fingers
for dinner preparation such as for tossing the
salad for which you wear special gloves made for
salad tossing from the drawer below the drawer
with the everyday silver which is made not of
silver but stainless steel Charles and have I told
you dear Wanda the cousin's cleaning lady not
Paca but the smaller one Conchita throws the
cookies out the window if you eat one too soon?

Mrs. Fa with her eyewear tucked under her chin

marches past in the dining room pushing a car
at the end of a stick of which the wheels make
a clackety gurgle Charles Wanda the noise of
somebody drowning. The older doctor's daughter
pays me no mind but the daughter in the middle
dear Wanda's same age is covetous yes she wants
my little room she likes the slant of the ceiling
if I am ever no longer employed in this house
such as for weeping too copiously and also too
often the girl will sleep most certainly most
proprietarily where I lie sleeping even one day a
boyfriend she'll take him there plus she covets a
skirt made of just one remnant of left over dining
room curtain fabric not the fabric made of glass
the fabric made of watery deep blue flowers the
flowers floating in blues the flowers steeped in
cool water but dear Wanda I'm sewing your skirt
first.

TARNISH

Unlike rust tarnish is self limiting. Whatever. The
doctor's daughter has no clue what self limiting
means perhaps it needs a hyphen perhaps tarnish
is unable to stop itself from tarnishing from not
letting one see what is required to be seen in
it to be understood by seeing it such as really
it doesn't matter so much the spirit in which
something happens as that it happens at all. To
someone. Right? Such as gazing over dinner at the
meat slicer asking how it passed the day like what
it did/does/do all day and what tomorrow.

The doctor the father the dad is dead the
doctor's wife also the mom is dead they're
interned in a wall atop a hill of many graves a
star carved into stone at which bugles play the
rings still on her fingers not one but maybe two
of them. Maybe Cynthia is buried someplace now
too there's no method of knowing since she had

no last name because she was/is only named
Cynthia a wall of many flowers someplace on
Saint Vincent. Plus is it wrong? Wrong to imagine?
To put words into speech to make thoughts in
her mouth? Should she apologize the daughter
yes/no is she sorry?

The wall of graves also the star with its six
incised points might even be said to be beautiful
if you look at the mom and dad properly in it if
you stand before them properly if you can find
them in it if you kneel before it properly.

WEB SEARCH

Monday: Cynthia mother Wanda Wanda daughter Cynthia mother Wanda granddaughter Cynthia Wanda daughter Cynthia grandmother of daughter of Wanda of.

Tuesday: Cynthia daughter Wanda Saint Vincent the Grenadines Cynthia daughter Wanda husband Charles father Wanda Saint Vincent and the Grenadines and the and.

Wednesday: Wednesday day off. Or was it Thursday day off? Or? Except the sister the older sister the judge would say really does it matter? Except you can't text a judge in the middle of a Wednesday to ask was the day off Thursday or Wednesday. It was Wednesday it was Thursday there was mass in the morning which morning was mass she couldn't go she couldn't get there Cynthia couldn't but there is mass on the radio

is mass supposed to be capitalized? Catholic
Mass Catholic mass catholic mass catholic
Mass. Back and forth she paces Cynthia in the
doctor's study the room with the books listening
to mass/Mass on the doctor's radio the books with
markings in them scribbled by the wife in the
margins starting with when she was skinny and
yellow the brackets the explanation points the
question marks the OHs or is it ohs or is it oh's
or is it Oh's in even Portnoy's Complaint which
the doctor's daughter was permitted to read at
age twelve and eleven even Naked Came the
Stranger even Kinsey she read or was it Masters
and Johnson for there were only two books the
doctor's daughter was forbidden to open to read
to sit down with Malcolm X and Eldridge Cleaver
it was said those two books would frighten the
daughter she was permitted to examine only the
spines of them reading over and over the titles
the names on them. But the speaker the radio
speaker hangs up in the corner where wall meets
ceiling a giant dark head tilting at the crisscross

of threads forming Cynthia's hairnet as she paces
to and fro the threads of mass/Mass reaching
musically for and around her which is at least how it
should be if you can't get to church if you don't
have a car you can cry if you want if there is no
one to drive you the doctor's daughter couldn't
drive her she wasn't even yet eleven had she
been sixteen she might have or at least so much
as asked but possibly not since that's how it was
the way it really was/is except it really doesn't
matter doesn't/does it anymore is/isn't a thing
to be sorry about and weep and apologize over
but if only she might find Wanda dear Wanda an
embrace might be or might not be possible a gift
of the several left behind rings she tries on where
she keeps them all jumbled up in their velvety
boxes they always fit they never don't they're
never lost never missing just where she finds
them where they belong.

Thursday: Private Eye The Grenadines Private
Investigator Saint Vincent and the or is it The/the

Grenadines or is it Cinthia never Cynthia not?

Friday: Births Saint Vincent The/the Grenadines Cynthia/Cinthia Charles' daughter Wanda deaths Saint Vincent the/The Grenadines deaths Charles' wife Cinthia Cynthia's husband Charles daughter Wanda deaths husband Charles daughter Wanda.

Almost: Dr. Wanda from The Grenadines Saint Vincent from Saint Grenadines Cynthia mother father Charles Dr. Wanda from The Grenadines Milton Cato Memorial Hospital Arnos Vale Medical Chateaubelaire Hospital nurse surgeon administrator insurance specialist financial counselor patient customer service Wanda the/The Grenadines urgent care mental health pediatric urgent Wanda.

Also: Also search Saint Vincent and the Grenadines Community College Friends 1979 also Saint Vincent and the Grenadines Community College Friends 1980 also Saint

Vincent and The Grenadines Community
College Friends 1982 also Saint Vincent and
The Grenadines Community College Friends
1974 also Saint Vincent and the/The Grenadines
Community College Friends 1981 also search
also not search also.

CYNTHIA

Dear Wanda I live in the little room.

The little room is upstairs between the playroom and the attic the playroom is where I put away toys.

The family bedrooms are downstairs on both ends of the house three daughters down one hall master bedroom down the other.

The little room has slanted ceilings or rather only one ceiling with one silly big slant so when I stand up from reading your letters Wanda I all too often bang my head on it.

The house is two stories high dear Wanda but from the window in the little room the little dormer window it appears I'm looking out from a tower across the tops of a forest of trees the trees are too big here on Wedgewood Lane Wanda.

The dogs too Wanda.

Please write me a letter every day.

The middle daughter has never seen airmail
stationary she covets your penmanship she wants
to be friends it's neater than hers she means to
write you one day a missive in code she likes
to slice open the envelopes she likes to button
unbutton the top of my pen she likes the touch
of my hairnet likes to pat it and pluck it likes to
smooth likes to write likes to read all our letters.

When snow falls Wanda I'll send you a photo
from the middle daughter's camera she lost a
Super Ball in here last week in the little room
we haven't been able to find it also my hairpins
my bobby pins I'll need to buy new ones it's a
Swinger the camera it swings from her wrist it
makes the photos right there in her hands when

she takes them.

Dear Charles last night there came a knock at the door the front door of the house not the door in the back where we all six of us were sitting eating our suppers. I sit at the counter. They sit at the table. I sit facing away from them into the kitchen where they can look at the buttons at the back of my uniform Charles I need to button with care my hair looped neatly in the hair net.

I sit straight as can be on a high stool no chair a stool facing the meat slicer and when the doorbell rang I went to answer it Charles I think that's part of my job.

Nobody was there but then I saw that the storm door had been kicked in there was glass on the mat I let out a scream the doctor phoned the police.

Charles I don't like this airmail stationary it has
not enough room the page fills up too fast.

The police came with clipboards they didn't sit
on the couch they stood up with their clipboards
they wrote down the things that the doctor said.
The doctor's wife said the picture window in
the dining room has no curtains since the new
curtains are being sewn by Cynthia our maid.
The cops wrote this down too. People were
watching us eating she said. People stood outside
the window and watched us at our meal at our
dining room table the dog Candy didn't bark I
was crying Charles but the girls weren't crying
it was only me crying not even the doctor's wife
was crying.

The police asked is there a boyfriend? The
other police said the maid does the maid have
a boyfriend? They all turned their heads to
wonder. I told them no I do not I told them what
they'd believe I told them it's my husband Charles's

grandma's spirit who comes to kick at the door
some nights when she's lonely I told them what
they'd believe I told them she's lonesome I said she
never intended to break the glass she's a spirit I told
them some spirits kick glass some nights with no
intention of it breaking I told them what they would
believe they didn't write this down I told them
Charles you'll instruct your grandma never to come
here ever again.

Soon I was asked politely to go upstairs. The
policeman asked the doctor's wife to ask me
so she asked me politely since she always asks
politely so I went upstairs politely.

I sat on my bed in the little room Charles not
in the playroom. I didn't feel like sewing curtains
even skirts dear Wanda I'll feel like sewing skirts
again tomorrow I hope. Also Charles I think I'm
now taller than you since when I finally stood up
from my bed in the little room I said to myself
now don't hit your head on that awful slanted

ceiling but still Wanda I did I still do I always do still always hit my head on it Charles.

TRAIN RIDE W/ APOLOGIES

At thirteen the doctor's daughter boards a train out of Huntington Station on her way to the city to visit friends from sleepaway camp who consider her a mama's girl. She only rarely rides the train and hardly ever alone but she's not ill at ease unless priding herself on being not ill at ease means she is ill at ease. She knows to change in Jamaica disembark at Penn Station and show her ticket when required an act she enjoys handing over the ticket to show she's paid up.

She takes a seat at the window so as to gaze at her reflection not appraising only philosophical enjoying the way there appear to be two of her one on a train but the other outside amid horse farms and dress shops and flat walled fish ponds gliding by. In the seat next to hers sits a man in a wool plaid shirt with a frayed orange collar who appears to her always in profile even now a half

century later their two silhouettes hers white his
black aligned in clamorous repose.

Complimented once for having excellent posture
more upright than her sisters' the girl sits up tall
for a five foot one and a half inch person and
as if she has already subjected herself to those
sadistic Pilates classes she holds her limbs flush
with the plane of her body her bag at rest on
one leg the strap over her shoulder both hands
in her lap. The train bypasses Roslyn en route to
Jamaica. She has camp friends from Roslyn who
play acoustic guitars and sing Phil Ochs songs
around murmurous campfires in backyard circles
on Saturday nights which appeals to her as being
a more enviable manner of being Jewish than she
herself is learning by her agnostic parents further
east on Long Island where Catholics live. When
she complains of this her mom the doctor's wife
answers certainly and where they go to school in
Roslyn all the kids are like them Jewish and they
hardly ever see a kid not to mention a grownup

hardly even a dog or a goldfish who isn't just like
them Jewish a liberal who adores Pete Seeger
just like you is that what you want? Which shuts
the daughter right up by putting her in fond mind
of the Bodillys and the Flanagans classmates of
hers whose comely moms pass whole days in
Simplicity housecoats while saying rosaries in the
event of dental appointments.

The Kellys wouldn't know Phil Ochs if he were a
guest at their own dinner table avowing in such
ugly times the only true protest is beauty.

Ochs died in a plane crash her Roslyn friends tell
her their tears stoppering their eyes so it's not
until she's sixty she'll learn from Wikipedia Ochs
hanged himself.

Maybe Wikipedia is incorrect.

Or else there is something impressionable about
her the too balanced core the too mindful range

of motion never to be jolted nor wrested apart
that make her friends link arms in protecting her
unless maybe the friends have been lied to by
their parents and maybe also their rabbi.

Her new bag or did she call it a purse then
resembles the travel kit she'll buy for Chuck five
decades later leather in the shape of a zipped
up shoebox. She likes the way the squared off
leather squats on her leg both hands in her lap
no book no food no water bottle everything
even the grownup shoulder strap inside the plane
of the body. Plus since wherever the doctor's
daughter sits or stands appears to be her
destination she's neither thirsty bored eager nor
impatient even knowing that when she reaches
Penn Station she'll take a cab to the penthouse
where since the parents are away there'll be boys
there too including one with whom she'll do her
first ever groping although having no brother to
catch sight of in hallways she'll have no clue which
part of him goes up that she can feel through

his underpants and which part goes down such as where does it start and where does it come undone?

But she is where she needs to be. She has everything she needs. She notes only a subliminal buzz in one leg the faintest signal as of a cell phone not yet invented.

One night her mom's brother not the one who never sat at his own mom's deathbed but the other one Milt phones her mom to enthuse about how while rounding a bend in Great Neck that morning his car struck the car being driven by his wife Aunt Evelyn or rather hers struck his. What are the odds Uncle Milt enthuses of two people intersecting such as by crashing into each other having already fallen in love with each other via fate happenstance or even two fenders rubbing against each other and both cars totaled? Later Suzie Milt's daughter will be in love with a black man and despite being Jewish

progressive a liberal they didn't use the word
progressive then a stone's throw from Roslyn Milt
for some time will spurn them. Meanwhile that
vibration the girl feels in her leg an improbable hum
as of something less material than locomotive more
mind than matter less tactile than incorporeal.

Come to think of it she called purses
pocketbooks then. Plus no one drank from water
bottles those bottles weren't invented yet.

The man next to her has not yet collided might
not ever collide but might or might not with her
pocketbook/purse via what might be the aura
of just one finger the orange cuff unfastened a
loose thread snaggling where a button should be
beneath which lies the zipper underneath which
lie three twenties and eleven ones or rather ten
ones plus one extra for good measure folded
inside a red madras wallet or did she call it a
change purse then with a brushed metal clasp the
dollars given the girl by her dad the doctor when

he dropped her at the train station that same morning.

Even though it's not usual for the doctor's daughter to be carrying seventy much less seventy one dollars in her change-purse/wallet/pocketbook/bag the dollars aren't things that hold her attention not even when she spends them like if she goes to a head shop she and her friends once she meets them in the city they'll ride a bus eat Chinese maybe purchase a Ferlinghetti chapbook and at the end of the day she'll keep whatever dollars are still in her wallet/change-purse/whatever since her dad never asks for them back again they will be hers her dollars.

Also is it wrong to put thoughts into his head the man practically dozing his eyes open then closing his fingers wobbling via the train's agitation the man in his waking moments wishing to protect her from her fears although she has no fears and in his sleeping moments dreaming and of his hand

just one finger in reach of the purse the smallest
fatherly finger but not the finger just the aura in
reach of the tab of the zipper or rather hovers
above where the zipper needs pushing not pulling
unfortunately she notes since pulling would be
much easier.

The train nears Jamaica then leaves behind
Hicksville the kindly fatherly fingers as of a well
worn glove meaning not to alarm her meaning
only instead to comfort her. Which they do.
She is. She is perfectly comfortable perfectly
interested observing sideways the man no longer
a stranger his young daughter her age at home
named Wanda although maybe it's wrong to put
names in his mouth since Wanda's also the name
of the doctor's daughter's family's fired live-in
maid Cynthia's daughter who lived with her
dad Charles Cynthia's husband in Saint Vincent
and the Grenadines two thousand and sixty
five miles away who hoped someday to pay for
medical school with the dollars earned by her

mom Cynthia if only Cynthia weren't fired for
being so homesick on Sunday mornings about
needing to serve the doctor's family's brunch of
puffy pancake topped with confectioners sugar
and the juice of two lemons instead of going to
church if she even could get there having no car.
Plus it's nearly impossible to avoid at all times the
wrong things to say or the wrong ways of saying
the right things to do but the daughter at least
likes to try such as by moving the pocketbook
sideways as if unconsciously just an inch or two
sideways away from his finger the finger jumping
in surprise although she dislikes jumping in books
and in stories things jumping in surprise happen
way too often more than in life or on trains or in
supermarkets. Like only recently she spoke the
name Emily aloud in the supermarket so pleased
was she to run into Emily one of the hardly any
black people to whom she's been introduced
over twenty five years of living here in Oshkosh
Wisconsin and in the presence of whom her shyness
makes itself felt as an awkward limb an extra elbow

that elbows its way in front of her to jumble up
the space between her and Emily except the
woman didn't answer didn't/doesn't jump in
surprise doesn't/didn't glance up from where she
scrutinized the label of a Manwich can indicating
either that it really isn't/wasn't Emily or that
the doctor's daughter's worries that it wasn't/
isn't Emily caused her to speak her greeting too
meekly to be heard.

They slip into his lap the offended fingers the
orange plaid cuff with the snaggled thread as side
by side he and the doctor's daughter ride the
rest of the way to Penn Station in silence less
comforting than before their quarrel unspoken
coming and going such as when did it start and
when might it come undone? Only first the
train stops so off they go first the man then the
girl just seconds apart amid other passengers
stepping either on or off between and around.

Goodbye she even bids the man now in her mind

your own daughter dear Wanda my exact same age whose name waves itself away whose name disappears itself her penmanship across the blue airmail letters is/was prettier than mine is it wrong to put words to put thoughts into Wanda/Cynthia isn't/is.

Still the doctor's daughter worries that this waxing over Wanda who maybe did go to medical school maybe even in St. Louis where she herself got her Bachelor's maybe even the dates intersecting maybe even the two of them passing each other once or twice on a sidewalk might suggest she is being ironical when really she's in earnest lamenting never having met Wanda hardly ever searched for Wanda hardly even on Facebook nor hardly Safari only twice or thrice times some days half hearted and some days whole hearted and only some days almost but not quite ever finds.

Is she ashamed? No. Will she apologize no is

she sorry no/yes she really isn't/is/won't she wouldn't/couldn't/might say only first the cabbie shouts from a rolled down window young lady it's customary to leave a tip. At which she unzips the bag unclasps the red plaid madras wallet hands over six ones or rather five ones plus one for good measure and wondered and still wonders is this too much?

ACKNOWLEDGMENTS

For careful readings, consultation, advise, kindness, and smarts, thanks to the judge, Sylvia LaMar… and Laurie Alberts, Leslie Ullman, and Deborah Schneider. Robin Marlowe's recollections filled in a gap or two I didn't know were there, and best brother-in-law Rod Mehling's technical assistance saved way too many days. To readers for the Robert C. Jones Short Prose Book Prize, the Slope Editions Book Prize, the Marie Alexander Poetry Series, the 42 Miles Press Poetry Award, and the Deborah Tall Lyric Essay Book Prize: your nods of encouragement gave me just the push I needed.

Finally, endless appreciation and gratitude go to Randall Brown at Matter Press for Compressed Creative Arts, whose email read, simply, "Read it, loved it, would love to publish it."
        Abby Frucht, 2020

ABOUT THE AUTHOR

Abby Frucht's first collection of stories, *Fruit of the Month,* won the Iowa Short Fiction Prize for 1987. She has since published a second collection of stories and 6 novels including *Licorice, Polly's Ghost,* and *A Well-Made Bed. Maids,* which tells the story of Abby's efforts to speak to and about the women employed by her parents as "maids" when she and her sisters were girls on Long Island in the 1960's, '70s, and 80's, is her first book of poetry. She lives in Wisconsin, and has served as mentor and advisor for 25 years at Vermont College of Fine Arts. You can find her and some of her online writings at http://www.abbyfrucht.net.